fine
art
photo s

Pig on a Platform   Nashville, Tennessee

Photography © 2002 Meryl Truett

Velvet Hammer Press

Contact: mtruett@comcast.net
        www.meryltruett.com

Silver prints of images are available.

ISBN:0-9724721-0-X

Design: Mandy Stinson

For my husband
John Dodge Meyer

Special Thanks: Rebecca Nolan,
Steve Bliss, Tom Fischer,
Sue Valentine, and Rhonda Arntsen.

And thank you to my mother,
Jean Knight Truett.

Thump Queen
and other Southern Anomalies

by Meryl Truett

Meryl Truett

I N T R O D U C T I O N

 Years ago driving through Luling, Texas (population 5080), a strange sign caught my eye. In the shape of a slice of watermelon, the sign read "Elect Stephany Cleaveland, June 10, Thump Queen." When I snapped the shutter of my old plastic Diana camera that day, I made a decision to document the South where a young girl desires to be crowned Thump Queen and reign over the watermelon harvest. A piece of plywood painted crudely with primitive lettering epitomizes the kind of southern imagery that I wanted to capture on film. I wanted to convey my vision of the naive, rural sensibility that is prevalent even in Southern cities, a connection of people to the land and the crops. These often overlooked, yet significant, details of everyday life make up the body and soul of this book.

Thump Queen   Luling, Texas

A R T I S T   S T A T E M E N T

Growing up in the South has given me a rare vantage point from which to observe the ever changing landscape of a region in transition. I am drawn to the images that are so familiar, yet so alien to me.

From crude back-roads signs to eccentric and sometimes humorous records of the quirky manifestations of Southern culture, my photographs capture a particular vision of vanishing iconography and a certain moment in time.

I am interested in documenting and cataloguing the remnants of a lost time and a lost way of life. My focus lies not with the mythical Old South of privileged Southern belles and gentlemen sipping mint juleps on white columned verandas, but with the authentic, hard-scrabble South of hand-scrawled signs stabbed into the piney-woods, make-shift barbecue joints with hickory smoke billowing from rickety chimneys, and the Mom and Pop meat'n'three restaurants that dot the less traveled crisscross highways. The South is a land where religion still holds on in the face of MTV, AOL, and Adult Video; a culture where economic necessity has lead to marvelous inventions of food, architecture, and "accidental" irony. From the rolling hills of Virginia to the tropical flats of Florida, the South is a fertile hunting ground for a disappearing America.

Through this book of photographs, I seek to collect, document, and preserve the objects, signs, and places of my memory before the complete infiltration of development and corporate mono-culture transforms the landscape forever.

Savannah, Georgia

Dudes' Bar B Q   Nashville, Tennessee

This Bloods 4 U   Nashville, Tennessee

Delta   Morning   Helena, Arkansas

Frank's Liquors   Memphis, Tennessee

Oysters   near Fredricksburg, Virginia

Holy Ghost Revival   St. Helena Island, South Carolina

Last Supper with Confederate Flag   Nashville, Tennessee

Stripe Drive-In   near Memphis, Tennessee

27th AVE Drive-in   North Miami, Florida

Sweetgrass Basket   near Pawley's Island, South Carolina

Chief Waki-Nomo   East Nashville, Tennessee

TeePee on Hwy. 17   near Winchester, Virginia

Hwy. 17 Truck   South of Fredricksburg, Virginia

No One under 21   Shell Point, South Carolina

Live Eels   Shell Point, South Carolina

Cross on a Tree   Savannah, Georgia

Apartments Trailer Park   near Eulonia, Georgia

El Rocko   Savannah, Georgia

Fish   Atlanta, Georgia

Ruffin's Pond   near Fredricksburg, Virginia

Son & Mother   Nashville, Tennessee

Defy Medeocrity (sic)   Nashville, Tennessee

Pool Cold Beer Seafood   near Hardeeville, South Carolina

Flamingo Lounge   Nashville, Tennessee

Cotton Field with Shadow Mason, Tennessee

Robert's Boot Barn   Nashville, Tennessee

Ernest Tubb Record Shop   Nashville, Tennessee

Drive-in Screen   near Key West, Florida

Same Great Staff   Georgia-South Carolina Border

Sacred Cow   near Frogmore, South Carolina

Fire Escape   Charleston, South Carolina

Dr. Robert Parks, founder, The Mercy of Jesus Synagogue   Charleston

Get Right with God   somewhere in Alabama

Soul Palace   Lady's Island, South Carolina

Velvet Elvis   Nashville, Tennessee

Why Jesus   Gardens Corner, South Carolina

Heart Tree   Savannah, Georgia

Shotgun Barrel   Georgia/South Carolina Border

Bad Antiques   Ravenel, South Carolina

Cow on Roof   near Suffolk, Virginia

Cow on a Stick   Hwy. 1, Lola, Mississippi

Dixie Bar B Q   Athens, Georgia

Elvis Meat 'N' Three   Memphis, Tennessee

Bad Bob   James Island, South Carolina

Big Skate   Gold Vein, Virginia

Merry Xmas DJ   Nashville, Tennessee

Home of Catfish Hunter   Hertford, North Carolina

Kudzu Barn   near Tappahanock, Virginia

Free Trip   Sheldon, South Carolina

Heaven   Monterey, Tennessee

Lightning Burger Bear   Memphis, Tennessee

The Last Time Around   Savannah, Georgia

Repent Final Warning   Homestead, Tennessee

B I O G R A P H Y

MERYL TRUETT is a fine art and editorial photographer whose work is exhibited and collected nationwide. She holds a Master of Fine Arts degree in Photography from Savannah College of Art and Design and a Master's degree in Media Arts from the University of South Carolina with additional art training in France. She has received numerous awards including an Individual Artist Fellowship from the Tennessee Arts Commission.

Among the many publications featuring her photographs are: <u>Darkroom Magazine</u>, <u>Petersen's Photographic</u>, <u>Camera Austria</u>, <u>Nashville Scene</u>, <u>Nashville Life</u>, <u>The Vanderbilt Review</u>, <u>Connect Savannah</u>, <u>Savannah Magazine</u>, and <u>Creative Loafing of Savannah</u>. <u>Fall Harvests</u>, a book illustrated with her photographs was published in 1998. <u>Spring Pleasures</u> was released in 1999.

Truett's clients include Polygram Records, Sony Music, and the Ingram Group. Her works are represented in the private collections of Roseanne Cash, Chet Atkins, Ashley Judd, Delbert Mann, Tom Schulman, Vanderbilt University, BellSouth Corporation, and the University of South Carolina.

Meryl lives in Savannah with her husband, artist John Dodge Meyer. Their family includes three extremely spoiled dogs and two shamefully privileged cats.